Crystals, crystals everywhere

Did you know that crystals are all around you? There are crystals in your kitchen in the form of sugar and salt. There are crystals at the beach in the form of sand. Mountains are full of crystals, and crystals are used in many types of tools from pencils to computers.

Turn the page and enter the incredible world of crystals. Then try making your own rock-candy crystals by following the instructions on pages 13–16. But remember—even though you can eat the sugar crystals you will make, you cannot eat other kinds of crystals.

What is a crystal?

A *crystal* is a piece of solid matter with smooth, flat surfaces that form naturally. The atoms of the solid matter are arranged in an orderly pattern that repeats over and over again. It is this identical pattern that gives a crystal its shape.

The word *crystal* comes from a Greek word meaning "clear ice." Ancient people thought that colorless quartz was actually ice that had hardened so much it could not melt. In fact, quartz is a mineral that forms crystals, while ice is water frozen into a crystal solid. Quartz and ice look similar, but they are not the same.

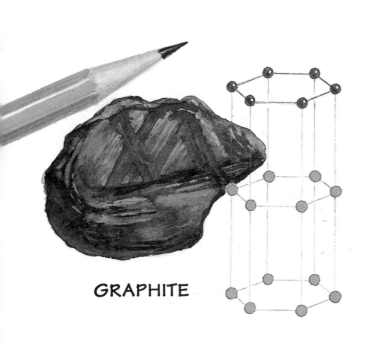

GRAPHITE

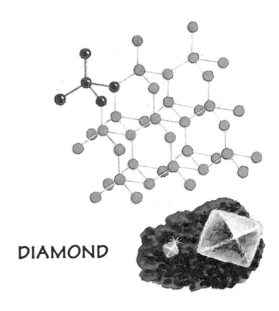

DIAMOND

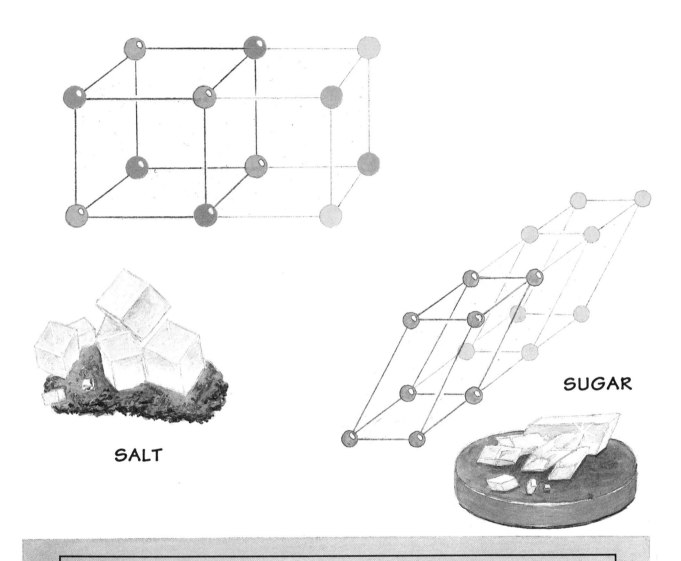

SALT

SUGAR

CRYSTAL FACT: Snowflakes are crystals. They are formed from water vapor, which crystallizes around tiny particles called ice nuclei (NEW-klee-eye).

How does nature form crystals?

Most crystals start out as molten rock, or *lava*, deep within the earth. Pressure within the earth forces the molten rock upward toward the surface. As the rock is pushed up, some of it becomes trapped in cracks and crevices in the earth's crust. Over time, the molten rock cools and hardens and crystals form.

When crystals form, we say they "grow." Crystals are not alive, so they do not grow in the same way that people, plants, and animals do. However, they do grow in the sense that they start out small and get bigger as more crystal layers are added to the outside of the crystal.

Nature also grows crystals in caves in the form of *stalactites* and *stalagmites*. These formations result when water, containing the mineral *calcite*, drips into the cave. As the water drips, it evaporates, leaving a deposit of crystal formations behind.

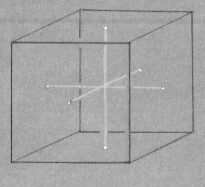

CUBIC

MONOCLINIC
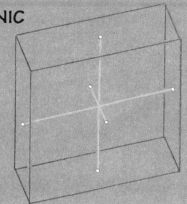

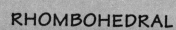

RHOMBOHEDRAL

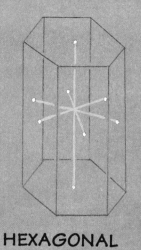

HEXAGONAL

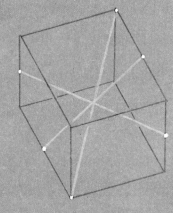

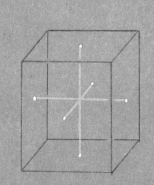

TETRAGONAL

TRICLINIC

ORTHORHOMBIC

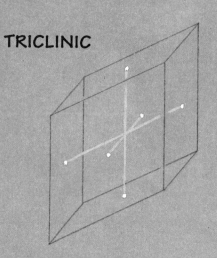

6

How are crystals classified?

The smallest portion of a crystal that shows the orderly pattern of atoms is called a *unit cell*. The shape of the unit cell and the way the unit cells are arranged determines the shape of the crystal.

Crystals are classified according to the shapes of their unit cells. There are seven possible shapes: *cubic* (or *isometric*), *triclinic*, *tetragonal*, *rhombohedral*, *orthorhombic*, *monoclinic*, and *hexagonal*.

A crystal's *habit*—the word used to refer to its external appearance—may not be the same as the shape of its unit cells. This is because the crystal grows in various directions, depending on the space it has and other factors.

CRYSTAL FACT:
The inside structure of crystals was unknown until 1912, when scientist Max Theodor von Laue used an X-ray beam to study the arrangement of atoms within crystals.

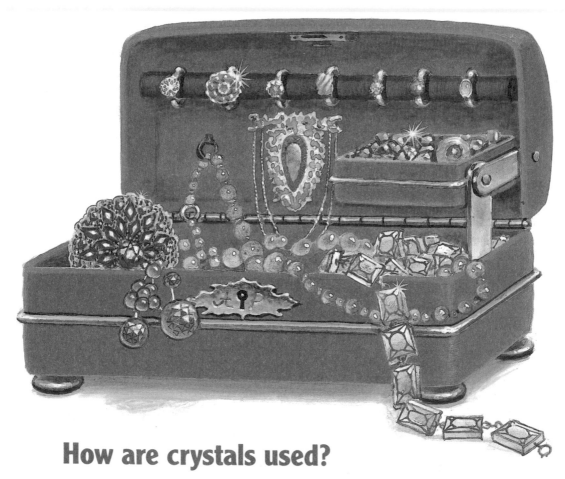

How are crystals used?

Crystals have many uses. Some crystals, such as diamonds, rubies, emeralds, and opals, are called *gemstones*. These crystals are valuable because they are rare, they reflect light in pleasing ways, and they can be placed in settings and worn as jewelry.

Crystals are also used in machinery, electronics, medicine, and communications. In fact, much of modern technology depends on the use of crystals.

♦ Diamond crystals, because of their great hardness, make excellent cutting tools such as rock drills.

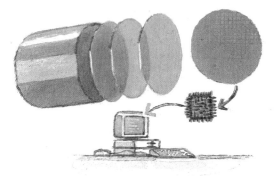

♦ Silicon crystals, which can be sliced into very thin wafers, form the basis of computer technology.

♦ Quartz, which vibrates, is used in watches.

♦ Crystals of silver salts, which are light-sensitive, make photography possible.

CRYSTAL FACT: Liquid crystals, which flow like liquid but have some of the properties of crystals, are used in calculators for number displays.

How can I grow crystals at home?

If you have ever seen a piece of rock candy, you may know that it is made up of large-sized sugar crystals—crystals that are larger than those in your sugar jar. To grow large crystals from sugar, all you need are a few simple ingredients and some time. When you are ready, turn to pages 13–16 for step-by-step instructions on how to grow your own sugar crystals.

The easiest way to grow crystals at home is to prepare a *solution*. A solution is made by dissolving a solid in a liquid. When a solid, such as sugar, dissolves in a liquid, such as water, the crystals of the solid break up into individual molecules. The sugar molecules become distributed among the water molecules, and the sugar is said to be "in solution."

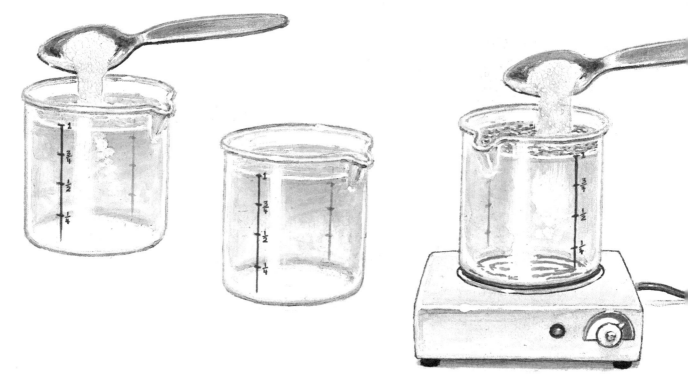

As you add more sugar to the solution, it continues to dissolve up to a point. At that point, it is not possible to dissolve any more sugar in the solution because the solution is *saturated*.

If you heat the saturated solution, you can add more sugar and it will dissolve. As the solution cools, it is able to hold less and less of the dissolved sugar. The result is a *supersaturated solution*. What happens to the extra sugar in a supersaturated solution? It comes out of solution and forms crystals.

> **WARNING:** The crystals described here are made from sugar and water and therefore can be eaten. NEVER EAT ANY OTHER CRYSTALS, even if they look like rock-candy crystals!

How can I grow extra-large rock-candy crystals?

Is adding more sugar to the saturated solution the only way to grow bigger rock-candy crystals? What if you took away some of the water from the solution? There wouldn't be enough water to keep all the sugar in the solution. More sugar would have to come out—sugar that could make your crystals grow even larger.

How can you take away some of the water? Think of a puddle after a rain shower. What happens to a puddle when it is exposed to the air? It dries up, or *evaporates*. In the same way, if you let some air into your sugar solution, some of the water will evaporate. The more water that evaporates, the less sugar the solution will be able to hold, and the larger your crystals will grow.

CRYSTAL FACT: The largest known crystals are formed by a mineral called *microcline*. Single crystals weighing more than 2,000 tons (1,820 metric tons) have been discovered.

Instructions for growing sugar crystals

IMPORTANT: Do not try this experiment yourself. Ask an adult to help you, especially with the first two steps.

What you'll need:

wooden stick
plastic disc
crystal-coloring tablet
measuring cups
granular cane sugar

saucepan
stove or hotplate
wooden spoon
pot holder
tall drinking glass

1. *Preparing the Solution.* Measure 2⅔ cups (.64 l) of sugar and set it aside. Measure 1 cup (.24 l) of water and pour it into the saucepan. If you would like your crystals to be red or green, select a crystal-coloring tablet and add it to the water. Put the saucepan on the stove or hot-plate and bring the water to a boil.

2. Once the water has started to boil, turn the heat down to medium and add the sugar you measured out earlier. Stir the mixture with the wooden spoon for 10–15 minutes until all the sugar has dissolved and the solution looks clear. Using the pot holder, remove the pan from the burner. Set the solution aside and allow it to cool for at least 1/2 hour, stirring it from time to time.

3. *Preparing the Glass.* While the solution cools, take one wooden stick and push it through the hole in the center of the plastic disc. Set the disc on top of the drinking glass. Adjust the length of the stick so that the end inside the glass is about 1 inch (2.54 cm) from the bottom of the glass.

4. *Preparing to Grow Crystals.* Once the solution has cooled, remove the disc with the stick from the glass and pour the solution into the glass. Use only as much solution as you need to fill the glass to about 1 inch (2.54 cm) from the top. (Discard the rest or use it for a second crystal-growing experiment with a disc you've cut from cardboard.) Then replace the disc and stick, being sure to position the stick as before. Put the glass in a safe place where it won't be disturbed while the crystals grow.

5. *Growing Crystals.* After about a day, you'll notice tiny crystals forming along the length of the stick. With every passing day, more sugar will come out of the solution and attach to the crystals on the stick, making the crystals grow larger and larger.

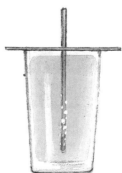

After about a week, the crystals will stop growing and will be ready to eat.

6. *Growing Even Larger Crystals.* If you wish to grow even larger crystals, carefully lift the plastic disc and place two unsharpened pencils underneath, so the disc is resting on the pencils instead of resting on the top of the glass. This will permit air to get into the glass and allow the water to evaporate. Check your crystals again after three or four days. If there is any solution left in the glass, pour it out and put the disc with the stick back in the glass to dry out overnight. The next day your crystals will be ready to eat. Enjoy!

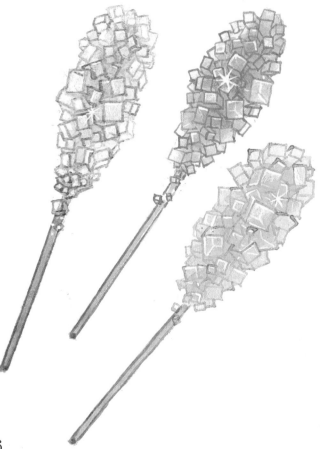